◄ NATIVE AMERICAN PEOPLE ►

THE
YAKAMA

by Edward Ricciuti

Illustrated by Richard Smolinski

ROURKE PUBLICATIONS, INC.

VERO BEACH, FLORIDA 32964

CONTENTS

A Note from the Publisher

In 1994 a tribal resolution of the Yakama nation was passed to revert the spelling of the tribe's name from "Yakima" to "Yakama"—the spelling used in an 1855 treaty between the Yakama and the U.S. government.

Library of Congress Cataloging-in-Publication Data

Ricciuti, Edward R.
    The Yakama / by Edward Ricciuti; illustrated by Richard Smolinski.
        p.   cm. — (Native American people)
    Includes index.
    Summary: Examines the history, traditional lifestyle, and current situation of the Yakama peoples of the Columbia Plateau.
    ISBN 0-86625-604-0
    1. Yakama Indians—History—Juvenile literature.
2. Yakama Indians—Social life and customs—Juvenile literature. [1. Yakama Indians. 2. Indians of North America—Washington (State).] I. Smolinski, Dick, ill. II. Title. III. Series.
E99.Y2R53 1997
973'.049741—dc21   97-5899
                                      CIP
                                      AC

Introduction

For many years, archaeologists—and other people who study early Native American cultures—believed that the first humans to live in the Americas arrived in Alaska from Siberia between 11,000 and 12,000 years ago. Stone spear points and other artifacts dating to that time were discovered in many parts of the Americas.

The first Americans probably arrived by way of a vast bridge of land between Siberia and Alaska. The land link emerged from the sea when Ice Age glaciers lowered the level of the world's oceans.

The first migration across the bridge was most likely an accident. It appears that bands of hunters from Asia followed herds of mammoths, giant bison, and other Ice Age game that roamed the 1,000-mile-wide bridge. Over a long time—perhaps thousands of years—some of the hunters arrived in Alaska.

Many scholars now suggest that the first Americans may have arrived in North America as early as 30,000 or even 50,000 years ago. Some of these early Americans may not have crossed the bridge to the New World. They may have arrived by boat, working their way down the west coasts of North America and South America.

In support of this theory, scientists who study language or genetics (the study of the inherited similarities and differences found in living things) believe that there may have been many migrations of people over the bridge to North America. There are about 200 different Native American languages, which vary greatly. In addition to speaking different languages, groups of Native Americans can look as physically different as, for example, Italians and Swedes. These facts lead some scientists to suspect that multiple migrations started in different parts of Asia. If this is true, then Native Americans descend not from one people, but from many.

After they arrived in Alaska, different groups of early Americans fanned out over North America and South America. They inhabited almost every corner of these two continents, from the shores of the Arctic Ocean in the north to Tierra del Fuego, at the southern tip of South America. Over this immense area, there were many different environments, which changed over time. Early Americans adapted to these environments and changed with them.

In what is now Mexico, some Native Americans built great cities and developed agriculture. Farming spread north. So did the concentration of people in large communities, which was the result of successful farming. In other regions of the Americas, agriculture was not as important. Wild animals and plants were the main sources of food for native hunters and gatherers, like the Native American people of the Columbia Plateau. This region was home to many different tribes, one of which was the Yakama tribe.

Origins of the Yakama

The Columbia Plateau lies between the Rocky Mountains to the east and the Cascades Mountains to the west. The Plateau includes most of central and eastern Washington as well as parts of southern British Columbia, Oregon, Idaho, and Montana. The Plateau is drained by two great river systems: the Fraser in Canada, and the Columbia in the United States. Unlike the arid Great Basin region to the south, the Plateau receives moderate rainfall, which supports grasslands and sagebrush. To the west, forests grow on the slopes of the Cascades.

Salmon once migrated up the Fraser and Columbia River systems to spawn, and they were a major source of food for all Native Americans of the Plateau, including the Yakama. The Yakama tribe also hunted game, and they gathered edible plants on the plains of the Plateau and in the mountain forests.

There are many indications that the ancestors of the Yakama came to the Plateau region a long time ago. Scientists have found evidence that Yakama may have lived there 12,000 years ago. About 4,000 years ago, other groups of people began moving into the Plateau from the north and from the south. Within another thousand years, the Plateau peoples were beginning to form permanent villages, where they lived during the winter months. In warmer weather, they left their permanent villages and travelled in search of food. Many of the Plateau tribes were closely related to the Yakama, and they were also divided into bands. These tribes all spoke the same language, called Sahaptin, although with slight variations.

Homes in the Plateau were similar to a type of housing still used sometimes by the Yakama. Each of these dwellings, called an "earth lodge," was constructed over a 3-foot-deep pit in the ground. As a result, the lodge was partially underground. Posts were sunk into the floor and attached to rafters, which supported the cone-shaped roof. The frame of the earth lodge was covered with willow branches, reeds, grass, and mud. A hole was left at the top of the roof in order to allow smoke to escape and light to enter the home. Some of these dwellings were more than 30 feet in diameter.

In the 1700s, the Yakama's way of life began to change rapidly, particularly after they adopted the horse as a means of transportation. Horses were originally brought to North America in the 1500s by the Spanish. During the seventeenth century, the Pueblo tribes of the Southwest began trading them with other Native Americans. Horses were soon being used as a means of transportation throughout western North America. In the early 1700s, the Yakama obtained horses from the neighboring Shoshone, who were horse traders. The Yakama quickly gained fame as skilled horse breeders and horsemen.

By the late 1700s, the Yakama were riding east to hunt bison, also known as buffalo, on the Great Plains. There, they came into contact with the Plains tribes and adopted many of their ways. The Yakama gave up their traditional clothing made out of plant material in favor of the buckskins worn by the Native Americans of the Plains. The Yakama also began making *tipis*, which were portable and could be brought along on hunting and fishing trips. The *tipis* were made out of lodgepole pine trunks wrapped in mats made of tule rushes, which grew in the marshes. The mats were tied together by hemp fibers or rawhide. These tule-mat *tipis* were eventually replaced by deerhide *tipis*, which had a similar structure.

Before the Yakama acquired horses and made contact with white Europeans, they numbered several thousand people—as many as 7,000 according to some estimates. At that time, the tribe was scattered in about fifty small villages that were located along rivers. Some of these villages had only a few dozen residents, while others had several hundred. Several villages had more than 1,000 inhabitants.

During the 1800s, the Yakama began building other types of permanent dwellings in addition to earth lodges.

Opposite: The Yakama lived in **tipis** *during the spring and summer months.*
Below: The winter lodges were permanent dwellings that were shared by several families.

The most common permanent home was the winter lodge. It had a slanting roof similar in appearance to the modern A-frame building. The frame of the winter lodge was made out of wooden poles, and these were covered with tule mats. Each of these homes reached up to 100 feet in length, and it was shared by several families. A different section of the house was allotted to each family. People slept next to the walls, and fires were built along the center of the floor. The smoke escaped through openings in the peak of the roof.

Daily Life

The daily life of the Yakama varied according to the season. During the winter, they stayed in their permanent villages. As spring approached, they moved to temporary encampments along the Columbia River. There, they fished for salmon that were swimming upstream to spawn. Later in the year, the Yakama headed for places where they could dig for edible plant roots. Next came another fishing expedition. In midsummer, the Yakama moved

Every spring, Yakama families moved close to the Columbia River, where they fished for salmon.

into areas where wild plants and game were plentiful. In late summer and early fall, they gathered berries. Some of the best areas to pick them were in the mountains, especially one that the Yakama called *Pahto*, which today is known as Mount Adams.

Socializing was an important aspect of Yakama village life. In the summer, the Yakama attended large gatherings where they feasted, played games, and traded goods with one another. They also traded with other tribes, especially those from the West Coast of North America. The Native Americans of the Northwest, like many along the East Coast, used seashells as a form of currency as well as for decorative purposes.

Family Life

The Yakama lived primarily in extended families. Children, parents, and grandparents all shared one lodge. Like many other Native American peoples, the relationships between Yakama grandparents and their grandchildren were especially close. Grandparents taught the children to respect others and explained Yakama traditions to them.

"Mother Nature is our teacher" was a popular Yakama saying. Adults taught children how to behave properly using examples from the animal kingdom. The behavior of quail, for example, illustrated the importance of family unity. Quail mothers stayed close to their young while the fathers guarded them. According to the Yakama, this showed that family unity led to safety. A different lesson was provided by the turtle, which was always at home because it lived in its shell. The

Yakama believed that like the turtle, a person should always feel at home no matter how the seasons changed.

Yakama mothers carried their infants on cradle boards. A baby was strapped to this wooden board, which could be carried on the mother's back or propped on the ground while she was busy with work.

Men and women performed different tasks, which were learned at a young age. While the men hunted and fished, the women gathered plants, made clothing, and prepared food. After the Yakama acquired horses, the men took charge of breeding and herding the animals. The women also made different kinds of baskets, which were used for a variety of purposes, such as food storage. Yakama women were among the most skilled of all Native Americans in basket making. They wove beautiful baskets from plant materials, such as grass, hemp, and cedar roots. Many of these baskets were elaborately decorated with beads.

Every Yakama woman kept a "time ball," or *ititamat*, which was a record of her life. These balls were made out of hemp fiber string. Girls began winding *ititamats* when they entered their teenage years. Throughout their lives, they marked important events, such as their first courtship, by placing a knot or bead on the string. The balls grew larger with time and were usually divided for easier handling.

Yakama children learned much about their people's traditions from their grandparents.

The Yakama were well known throughout the
region for their superb horsemanship, and for
the fine horses they bred.

13

Yakama women dug the bulbs of the camass plant, which they used for food.

Food

The Plateau people had an abundance of wild plants and animals available to them for food. They were fortunate to live in a region that included so many different types of natural environments—rivers, marshes, grasslands, forests, and mountains. Salmon and other fish were plentiful, as were edible roots, bulbs, and wild berries, which were staples of the Yakama diet. Women gathered the sweet-tasting bulbs of camass, a member of the lily family, and they dug edible roots from the ground using sharp, curved sticks. The meat of deer, elk, mountain sheep, birds, and eventually bison, were also part of the Yakama diet.

The Yakama worked hard to prepare and store food for the winter months. Salmon filets were dried on racks over fires, and they were stored that way or pounded into flour. Roots and bulbs were baked, or they were dried and pounded into powder. Berries were dried and often made into cakes. Sunflower seeds were also dried. Food was stored in beautiful baskets, which were kept in small storage houses or in pits lined with stones or bark. Some of these baskets were so tightly woven that they could be used to boil water.

Yakama children learned to dance at an early age so they could participate in the dances that celebrated the harvests.

15

Hunting and Fishing

The Yakama men were expert fishermen, and they used several different techniques to catch fish. From the shore, the men speared the fish with harpoons, often while standing on wooden platforms. They also snagged fish with gaffs (hooks with handles) and caught them in nets or seines (small nets). The Yakama built weirs, or dam-like structures made of sticks, so that they could net and spear the fish more easily. Every year, for centuries, thousands of Yakama gathered at prime salmon-fishing spots. The most important of these fishing grounds was Celilo Falls, located on the Columbia River in what is now Oregon. This fishery disappeared in the 1950s after a dam was built there.

The Yakama were also hunters, and their principal hunting weapon was the bow and arrow. The men hunted deer and other game animals on foot. After they obtained horses, the Yakama also hunted bison while on horseback, using bows and arrows. Riders would circle around and then ride into a bison herd, selecting their prey, and shooting them with arrows. Once the bison were killed, skinned, and butchered, the meat and hides were sent back to the village.

The Yakama used a variety of implements, as shown here, for hunting and fishing.

*During salmon season, Yakama fishermen used
nets to catch the fish as they swam upstream.*

17

Political and Social Organization

Yakama political and social structure was simple and effective. Its basis was the extended family unit. Most of the families within a village were related to each other in some way. Each village functioned independently and was headed by a chief. He was usually a man of proven intelligence who inherited the position from his father. A chief did not have total power over his village. His main function was to offer

Only the most skilled Yakama warriors were chosen to lead war parties.

guidance, and he was aided by a council of men chosen by members of the community. Decisions that affected the welfare of the entire village, such as organizing fishing expeditions or settling disputes, were made by the chief together with the council members. The council members in turn sought the advice of respected older women.

The council also managed relations with other Yakama villages. Different villages often worked together to gather food and fight enemies. Members of different villages who were linked by marriage would visit each other, sometimes for an entire winter.

Men and women with specialized skills—such as horse breeding, fighting, or basket weaving—also helped to provide leadership. A skilled warrior might be entrusted to head a war party, for example, while an expert hunter would help to organize deer and bison hunts.

Clothing

Before they adopted the buckskin garments of the Plains tribes, the Yakama made most of their clothing out of plant material, such as cedar bark strips. The men often wore robes, and the women wore tunics. The early Yakama also made capes and robes from deer and elk hides. By the time they first encountered white people in the nineteenth century, Yakama men were wearing shirts, leggings, and breechcloths made out of buckskin, and the women were wearing buckskin dresses. Their moccasins also were made out of buckskin, and their clothing was usually adorned with beads and shells. For decoration, the

This Yakama woman is wearing a traditional buckskin dress.

19

This man is dressed in a traditional buckskin shirt and leggings.

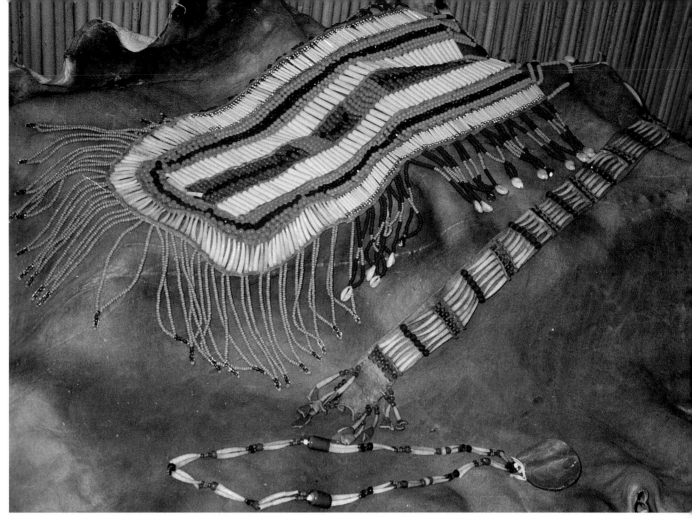

Colorful shell beads, or dentalium, decorate a wedding veil, a belt, and an abalone necklace.

Yakama wore painted arm and wrist bands, and the women wore shell earrings and fur ornaments in their hair.

On their heads, Yakama men and women wore beautiful cone-shaped hats. These were made from animal hides or plant fibers and were colorfully decorated with beads. The men wore feathered war bonnets, deer hair roaches (crests), and bison horn headdresses. These items, along with the Yakama's bone breastplates, originated with the Plains tribes.

Games

Like all Plateau people, the Yakama played several different types of games. The men competed with each other in races on horseback or on foot. Wrestling was another popular pastime among the men. Games of chance played with bones and sticks were enjoyed by both men and women.

One of the most popular games among Yakama women was called *shinny*. The game was a combination of hockey and soccer. Variations of it were played by many Native Americans. Two teams of between ten and twenty players each opposed one another on a field that was 75 yards long, and had a goal line at each end. The object of the game was to cross the opponent's goal line with a pair of balls that were tied together. The balls were about 4 inches in diameter and were made of stuffed deer hide. Each player carried a curved

Wrestling was a popular sport for the men. The mock combat increased their skills as hunters and warriors.

stick, which they used for hitting and pushing the balls down the field. Players could also kick the balls.

The first team to score a goal usually won the game. Sometimes, however, the losing team was given another chance. When this happened, the first team to score the tie-breaking goal was declared the winner. *Shinny* games often took hours to complete, and they were great social events for the Yakama. Games were sometimes scheduled every day for a period of several weeks.

Religious Life

The Yakama believed that a creator spirit formed them from the soil on which they lived. Like many other Native American people, the Yakama also believed in guardian spirits, which were usually related to nature and animals. As a child, each Yakama sought to contact his or her own guardian spirit through a ritual called a "vision quest." The same ritual was shared by Native American tribes throughout North America.

A young person on a vision quest fasted (went without food) and ventured out alone into the wilderness. There, he or she prayed for a dream that would reveal a guardian spirit. This process sometimes lasted for many days. When an individual returned from a successful quest, a shaman—spiritual leader—would interpret the young person's vision.

Visions were also experienced at village round dances, which were held regularly during the winter. While they danced, many of the Yakama went into trances and experienced dreams.

This doll, made from cedar bark, is an example of the Yakama's fine weaving skills.

Religious leaders from the village attended, and they provided the dancers with practical advice and spiritual guidance.

For the Yakama, religion was extremely personal. Every family unit had its own sweat house, where family members gathered to sing and meditate in the hot steam. Although the main purpose of the sweat house was spiritual, it also served as an important form of hygiene. The sweat house was round, and it was made out of bent willow branches that were covered with animal skins. The steam was made by pouring water over stones that had been warmed in a fire.

Early in the twentieth century, the Yakama added a new ritual to their religious practices. It was based on the teachings of the prophet Smohalla, who was a member of the neighboring Wanapam tribe. Smohalla urged all Native American peoples to retain their traditional way of life and to resist the influences of white culture.

A Yakama man finds solitude in his sweat house for meditation and prayer.

His Yakama followers worshipped together in rectangular buildings known as "long houses." During services, men and boys lined up along the northern wall of the building, while women and girls gathered along the southern wall. Ceremonies were conducted by a priest who sat at the western end. Services included dancing in place to drums, as well as chanting and speech-making by the adults. Some of them told of visions and preached about the importance of Native American traditions. Many Yakama, including those who practice Christian religions, still participate in long house ceremonies.

European Contact

White Americans first made contact with the Yakama in 1805, when the expedition of Meriwether Lewis and William Clark reached the Plateau region. The explorers found that many European trade items, such as cloth and metal goods, had already reached the Yakama through their trade with other Native American tribes.

By this time, the Yakama had also experienced some of the tragic consequences of contact between Native Americans and white people. During the late eighteenth century, smallpox and other illnesses began spreading east through the Columbia River valley and west from the Great Plains into Yakama territory. Epidemics of these diseases continued to affect the Yakama well into the nineteenth century, killing many of their people and even wiping out entire villages.

American and Canadian fur traders began entering the Plateau a few years after the Lewis and Clark expedition.

By 1811, the American-owned Pacific Fur Company established a base in the region, and this was soon followed by other trading posts. Yakama culture, already influenced by the arrival of the horse, began to change even more. Along with the other Plateau tribes, the Yakama traded with white people for firearms, cloth, and metal tools. When white traders began bringing cattle into the area, the Yakama took an interest in these animals. In 1840, the Yakama chief Kamiakin traded horses for cattle and established his own herd. Other chiefs soon did the same. During this time, the Yakama also learned to farm the land. By the early 1850s, they were raising corn, potatoes, squash, and other crops, and they were even irrigating their fields. Not long after the traders arrived, Christian missionaries began coming to the Plateau region. The missionaries included Roman Catholics, Methodists, and Presbyterians, and each denomination competed with the others for the allegiance of the Plateau people.

Still more changes were in store for the Yakama. By the mid-1830s, white settlers were moving westward along the Oregon Trail, passing Yakama territory on their way to the fertile Willamette Valley. During this period, Americans and British Canadians were both claiming rights to the Oregon Country, which included what is now Washington State. In 1846, after a bitter dispute, the present-day boundary between Canada and the United States was recognized. Under this agreement, Yakama lands came under the authority of the U.S. government. In 1853, the Oregon Country was divided into two parts: Oregon Territory and

The Yakama first met white Americans in 1805, when the Lewis and Clark expedition came to the Plateau region.

Washington Territory. Lands north of the Columbia River were made part of Washington Territory, which included areas of what are now Idaho and Montana. When this happened, Yakama lands lay within the boundaries of Washington Territory.

In 1854, a U.S. Army expedition moved onto Yakama lands to plan the construction of a railroad and a road. Meanwhile, the territorial government was developing plans to open Native American lands to white settlement. According to these plans, the tribes would sell their lands to the U. S. government and would then be relocated to reservations. These developments alarmed the Yakama, who began to unify their different villages under a small group of respected chiefs. One of the Yakama chiefs, Kamiakin, brought together leaders from most of the other Plateau tribes to form a council. The purpose of the council was to resist the territorial government's pressure on Native American lands.

The territorial government persisted, however, with its plans to relocate the Native Americans. In May 1855, the governor called a council of Plateau tribes near the present-day city of Walla Walla, Washington. At this meeting, government officials pressed Native American chiefs to sell their lands.

One by one, the tribes signed a treaty that took away their lands. On June 9, 1895, Kamiakin, along with the other Yakama chiefs, signed a treaty in Walla Walla that unified fourteen independent Native American groups into one nation. Some of these groups did not actually belong to the Yakama tribe, although they were closely related. By signing the treaty,

these tribes sold 16,900 square miles of land for just $200,000. They also agreed not to make war on other Native Americans except in self-defense. In return, the territorial government guaranteed to provide the Yakama with a reservation of 1,875 square miles in Washington Territory. They also agreed that white people would not be allowed on the reservation without permission from the Yakama.

The treaty did not take effect until four years later, however, when it was ratified by the U.S. Congress. In the meantime, it was illegal for whites to settle on Yakama lands. Nevertheless, white settlers began pouring into Yakama country, encouraged to do so by the territorial government. Miners came as well, on their way to newly discovered gold fields in what is now northeastern Washington. In 1855, fights broke out between the Yakama and the white intruders. Soon, the Yakama, aided by several other Plateau tribes, were at war with the U.S. Army. During the next three years, the Native Americans fought several battles against U.S. soldiers as well as territorial volunteer troops. Kamiakin was the most important Native American leader in what became known as the "Yakama Wars." For some time, the Yakama successfully resisted the attacks of the white armies. In September 1858, however, they surrendered after suffering a disastrous defeat. The U.S. government then executed twenty-four Native American leaders. Kamiakin, who had been wounded, escaped to Canada, where he died nineteen years later. In 1859, Congress finally ratified the Walla Walla treaty, and the Yakama moved onto their reservation.

The Yakama Today

Even after the Yakama settled on the reservation, they still faced pressure from the white population. One problem arose after Congress passed the Dawes Act in 1887. Under this law, reservation lands could no longer be owned collectively by tribes, but were to be divided up into allotments of 160 acres per family. Once the reservation was divided in this way, the U.S. government could negotiate to buy any remaining land. The Dawes Act was intended to help Native Americans become part of mainstream American society. Instead, it weakened the tribal unity that was central to their culture. Each year, more reservation land was divided up and redistributed to Native American individuals. The Yakama, however, persuaded the government not to take the reservation lands that remained after people received their allotments. In 1934, land allotment under the Dawes Act finally ended. Since the early 1900s, the Yakama have been purchasing land allotted

Spectators watch the "Treaty of 1855" parade in front of the Yakama Nation Cultural Heritage Center.

Many Yakama work for the lumber industry. This man is cutting wood for Yakama Forest Products.

to individuals and expanding the boundaries of their reservation. According to the Yakama, there are 5,859 members of the tribe living on the reservation, along with 3,146 members of other tribes. At least 800 more Yakama live on the outskirts.

Today, the Yakama nation is headed by a council of fourteen elected members. The tribal committees supervise fishing, health care, education, and other matters concerning the daily life of the people. Tribal income is generated mainly by timbering. Several other businesses and an industrial park are also in operation. Farming is another important economic resource for the Yakama. Their salmon fishery has been severely damaged over the years as a result of dam construction and river pollution. The tribe, however, has

begun to restore the fish, using money paid to them by the government for damages.

Tourism is also important to the Yakama. Besides bringing in money, it enables the Yakama to share their cultural heritage with other Americans. One of the reservation's major attractions is the Cultural Heritage Center. The history of the Yakama is presented in the center's museum, which has a restaurant that serves traditional food. Tourists who visit the reservation can even stay in an authentic *tipi.*

In the 1805 journals of Lewis and Clark, the Yakama were described as a people "of mild disposition and friendly disposed." The Yakama today are a busy, thriving people, and they invite others to visit them and learn about their rich and ancient culture.

Chronology

1775 A smallpox epidemic strikes Yakama for the first time.

1805 Lewis and Clark expedition makes contact with Yakama.

1811 Pacific Fur Company opens trading post on Columbia River.

1840 First Yakama cattle herd created.

1846 End of boundary dispute between the Americans and the British in Canada.

1853 Washington Territory established.

1854 Army expedition moves into Yakama country to plan road and railroad.

1855 Walla Walla treaty cedes Yakama lands to U.S. government; Yakama Wars begin.

1858 Yakama surrenders to U.S. government.

1859 Congress ratifies treaty and Yakama move onto reservation.

1887 Congress passes Dawes Act and allotment of reservation lands begins.

1934 Allotment of Native American lands ends.

1980 Yakama Cultural Heritage Center opens.

INDEX

Acknowledgments and Photo Credits
Cover and all artwork by Richard Smolinski.
All photographs courtesy of the Collection of the Yakama Nation Museum of the
confederated tribes and bands of the Yakama Indian Nation.
Map by Blackbirch Graphics, Inc.